Gigi Branch

Painting
Birds
on China

Marston House

I dedicate this book to my grandchildren, Shana and Sebastian

First published in 1998 by Marston House,
Marston Magna, Yeovil, BA22 8DH, UK

ISBN 1 899296 06 9

A CIP catalogue for this book
is available form the British Library

Acknowledgements
I am very grateful to my daughter Mandi for
bringing a fresh look to the designs by painting
her very original backgrounds to my birds.
All photographs by Alphabet & Image Ltd

Printed and bound by Regent Publishing Services, Hong Kong

Contents

Introduction

The historical background

In seventeenth-century Europe, before the arrival of porcelain, the tableware of the rich was silver and faience (white-glazed earthenware), with earthenware and pewter for the poor. Oriental porcelain was much prized for decorative purposes, as only the potteries of China and Japan at this time could manufacture this high-fired ceramic made from white clay. It was imported by wealthy Europeans, especially in Germany, in great quantities.

At this time, the nearest that European potteries could get to porcelain was Dutch Delft, which lacked the translucent quality so much admired in porcelain. But by the early eighteenth century a factory for the production of porcelain was established at Meissen, and in the next fifty years ones at Vienna, Berlin, Sevres, Chelsea, Worcester, Derby and other centres were producing their own finely modelled figures and decorated porcelain dishes.

The use of landscape and real or imaginary birds as subjects for decoration was widespread, and it is generally thought that the Japanese Kakiemon or Imari style was the original inspiration for European decorators. Exotic birds were first seen in Europe on Meissen porcelain, and were probably based on the real species in the Moritzbury aviaries in Germany, but under the influence of Oriental motifs such as the phoenix they became more and more fantastic. Among old Worcester pieces are some decorated with exotic birds in landscapes, said to have been done by a M Soqui, whose style resembles that of some Sevres painters. Many decorators at this time moved from factory to factory, and between countries, so styles within a factory's range were influenced by one major artist after another.

China painting today

Many of you will already have used my first book, *Painting on China in the French Style*, and will be familiar with the basic painting techniques, the materials you need, and the very varied results you can achieve. You will have mastered the basic brush strokes, learned how to line, make borders, gild, do relief work, groundlay, etc, and you will enjoy moving on to something a little different.

The subjects in this book are birds, set in landscapes, perched on stones or branches, and in flight. You can, of course, copy exactly any one of the 41 birds I show here, or you can change them - their size, shape of tail or beak, or colour - or set them in any of the 20 or so different backgrounds illustrated (these too can be reduced or extended to suit the shape of your piece) or you can set your birds among leaves and flowers taken from my first book. It is up to you!

You might like to visit some of the museums or great private collections and look at the fine porcelain decorated with birds - you will be thrilled and inspired by the wonderful craftsmanship to do your best and keep your own standards very high.

You can use any of the glazed blanks available from the suppliers listed at the end of this book. I have used some unusual ones in this book, but the choice is yours. You can paint in a group or class with other china painters, sharing a kiln, or you can paint at home, if you have your own kiln or can get your work fired locally. The most important thing is to enjoy yourself china painting, and don't forget to sign your work - it might be famous one day.

Tools, materials and firing temperatures

You will already have most of the tools and materials you require, so this is just a reminder. If in doubt about what some things are for, do consult my first book.

Brushes: I use (1) a large pointer brush with a head 1.5 cm long, 0.5 cm wide, for general painting, (2) a short small pointer, 0.8 cm long, 0.3 cm wide, and (3) a long fine pointer, 1.5 cm long, 0.2 cm wide for fine details. You can use a pen if you wish.

On-glaze powder paints: You must choose whatever colours you want, whether to match my designs or to suit your own taste.

Medium: Genuine vegetable turpentine and fat oil to mix the powder paints, *or* water-based medium and water (this is quick drying and should give you the same result as the oil-based medium). I do not recommend an open (slow-drying) medium if you wish to retain the strong colours and fine detail.

White tiles: Always useful, however experienced you are, for trying out new ideas, effects, etc, as well as to use as a palette for mixing paints.

You will also need: methylated spirits for cleaning the work surface before painting, a small palette knife for mixing paint, tracing paper for copying the designs and a soft graphite pencil or chinagraph pencil for drawing your design on to the porcelain, pen holder and nib, icing sugar (powdered) to mix with paint and water for quick-drying pen work, a lint-free cloth to wipe brushes, cocktail sticks to scratch out dry mistakes and lift off resist when doing groundlay, masking fluid, or resist (and a cheap pointer brush to apply it) to protect areas from groundlay, a flat nylon brush for groundlay, a sponge, cotton wool buds, a pipette, relief enamel, a well-lit working area, lamp and turntable.

Pottery blanks: there is an ever-increasing range available from suppliers (see list at the end of the book), ranging from dishes for the table or display, vases of all styles, shapes and sizes, tureens, urns, lidded jars and boxes. All are white glazed, already fired to about 1300°C/ 2370°F - far higher than you will be using - with a shiny surface ready for your decoration. You can get bone china, which is milk-white glazed porcelain composed of china clay, bone and feldspar,

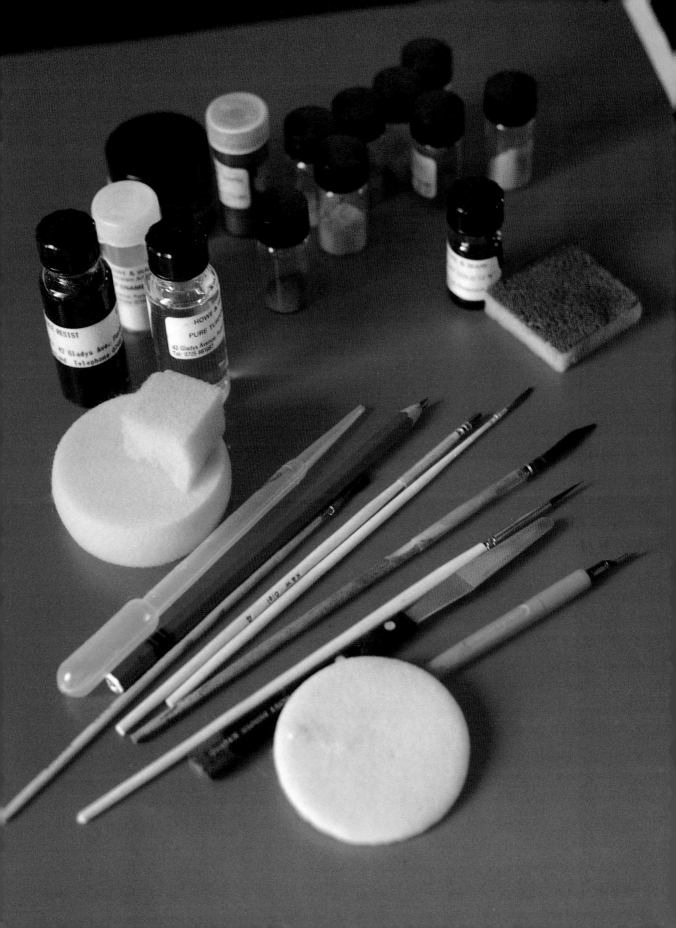

or porcelain, which is translucent when very thin, has a slight greyish tinge, and is made from china clay, quartz and feldspar. They require slightly different firing temperatures.

Firing temperatures

Painting colour on to white ware:
On porcelain - first firing: 820°C/1515°F second firing 800°C/1470°F
On bone china - first firing: 800°C/1470°F second firing: 780°C/1435°F

Painting gold:
On plain white porcelain or bone china: 780-760°C/1435-1400°F (but at 780°C if firing colour and gold at the same time).
On top of relief enamel: 740°C/ 1360°F
On top of painted design: 680-740°C/1250-1360°F

Relief enamel: 760-780°C/1360-1400°F

Groundlay: 825°C/1515°F for porcelain, 800°C/1470°F for bone china

Notes on some techniques

These will help if your memory needs refreshing, but if you feel unsure, consult my first book for more detailed instructions.

Gilding

You will need: burnishing gold, thin pointer brush (not to be used for other painting), gold thinners, burnishing pad or burnishing sand. You can buy Bright gold, which does not require burnishing as it dries very shiny.

Shake the gold in its medium vigorously before use. Add a drop of thinners as necessary to keep the gold running if it starts to dry. If you refer to the firing temperatures above, you will realise that you may need to fire gold twice, according to what it is being painted on.

Burnishing gold has a matt surface when it leaves the kiln, and needs to be made shiny by rubbing with a special pad or burnishing sand.

Remember when firing gold that the kiln must be well ventilated to allow fumes to escape. Leave the bung out, or the door slightly open, until the temperature reaches 400°C/750°F, then close the vent or door and let the temperature rise to the firing level.

Relief enamelling

You will need: white relief enamel, turpentine and fat oil, cocktail stick, thin pointer brush.

Mix the enamel with turps and fat oil until it becomes stringy, when you lift it with your palette knife. The enamel can be picked up with a cocktail stick or a brush but when dropped on to china it should keep a rounded profile. If drops spread it is too runny - let it dry a little; if it is spiky it is too dry - add a little oil and turps.

Relief in a tube: kits of ready-mixed enamel are now available and ready to be used from a tube, just as you would ice a cake, and these are useful. Instructions come with the kit.

Groundlay and masking

If you want your design to lie within a wide or narrow coloured border, you need to mask this border area very precisely to protect your design and give clear, clean edges for the coloured area. Masking fluid, or resist, should be painted on in a band about 15 mm wide either side (if necessary) of the reserved area. Apply it with an old brush, thickly, straight from the bottle and leave it to dry (you can speed this with a hairdryer). The colour is then painted and sponged on in the desired area and allowed to dry. The masking fluid can then be lifted off, like a sheet of thin rubber, with a cocktail stick. Carefully clean any marks in the white areas with a dry piece of cotton wool on a cocktail stick before firing.

12

How this book works

There is no 'right' way to paint birds; you will develop your own order of doing things. Above all, use the brushes and medium you are used to and are comfortable with. Most of the designs can be completed in two firings, but you can take more if you want, and for those pieces with gold or relief you will need extra firings anyway. I tend to paint the background and the birds at the same time, but if you prefer to complete one or other first, there is no reason why you should not do so.

For each design I give you:

1. **A drawing**, which you can trace and transfer to your chosen piece. Don't forget you can enlarge or reduce it on a photocopier, or flip the picture left to right simply by turning over your tracing.

2. **The first painting**, which represents the first firing. I personally like to start by thinly penning the eyes, the beaks and the feet with black paint, mixed with half the amount of icing (powdered) sugar and thinned with water to ink consistency, so that they are dry and will not move when I paint around them with my oil medium. (This does not apply, of course, if you use a water medium.) If there is a scene or large area to cover I use the large pointer brush and the colour mixed with turps and fat oil to apply a thin wash of colour. I keep it

body, followed by the head. For the wings, begin with the ends of the feathers and work your way up to the body.

3. **The second painting**, which represents the second firing. Now you can strengthen the colours as you think necessary, and paint the details such as the eyes and feathers with the fine pointer brush.

4. **A finished dish or vase showing the design**, which has sometimes been modified to suit the shape of the piece.

pale, as more colour can be added on subsequent firings.

Next I lightly paint the birds, using the smaller brushes, but only to the extent shown in the first illustration. If you paint quickly and confidently you may find it easier to complete one bird at a time. To do this you will have to premix all your colours. They will dry as you work and will need more turps. Start with the tail, then the

Details painted with the fine pointer brush in the second firing

Two birds on a flowering branch

This is an ideal design for beginners as the birds are very simple, and extra interest is added by the frame. The branches can be altered to fit any shape of plate, and this one is bone china.

Start with the first painting of the birds, following the illustration. I then put a border of masking fluid around the inside edge of the raised rim. I mixed two shades of blue with a little more fat oil than usual, applied the paint roughly in patches on the rim, then blended them with a dry soft brush. After removing the resist the dish was fired at 800°C/1470°C.

I then painted the details of the birds and added a band of bright gold around the outer and inner edges of the frame. The second firing was at 780°C/1435°F.

Lastly I covered the gold with dots of white relief enamel and fired for a third time, at 760°C/1400°F.

Birds on an oval casket

I designed this for a flat piece and had to make some adjustments to make it suit the curved, oval lid of the casket. I simplified the scene, adding more weight to the left and right by increasing the rocks, moving the tree and taking away the spray of flowers in the centre. I added birds from the design on page 43 to the sides of the base, using colours to match the lid.

Start with the scene, then the birds, in two firings as illustrated. The gilding was added at a third firing, because although it was possible to combine it with the second colour firing (as it is painted directly on to the white ground) it would have been very difficult to handle the piece with so much vulnerable wet paint. The third firing also allows you to add any further colour or details to the scene, if you think it necessary.

Crested bird on a pot-pourri

You can see the other side of this piece on page 6.

This had six firings in all, but don't let this put you off, as it is a lovely piece to decorate. I suggest you use several shades of green for the leaves as these form most of the background, and need to be a good colour foil for the birds.

Start by using masking fluid to reserve the space for the design and gold. I sponged a coat of groundlay of malachite

mixed with turps and fat oil on the lid, stem and base, and fired it at 800°C/1470°F. I then painted masking fluid over the same area again, put on a second coat of malachite, and fired a second time, again at 800°C/1470°F.

I then did the design of leaves and birds, in two firings, both at 780°C/1435°F, and finally two coats of burnishing gold, both at 760°/1400°C, making this a really rich piece.

Pheasant in a design of flowers

This is the same subject as you will see on page 6, but set in a pretty oval dish. See how important the white space is between the bird and the coloured border.

After completing the design and before firing the second time, I added the coloured border. I applied masking fluid in a band close to the unfired painting and the edge of the raised rim and also in a narrow band around the rim, following the relief on the dish. When it was dry I sponged the colour in the border area, let it dry, peeled off the making fluid, cleaned the white areas, and fired it.

Lastly I applied the gold and into the kiln it went for the third time, at 760°C/1400°F.

Two birds on a bramble

Because of the shape of this dish I lengthened the design by adding some branches between the birds and the top. Masking fluid protected the design and gave me an edge for the band of colour. I added dots on the colour band with a pen, and for a third firing painted the handles and the rim with burnishing gold, fired at 760°C/1400°F.

32

Crouching bird on pebbles

This vase can have a design on opposite sides, but I recommend that you complete and fire one side before starting the other, because it is difficult to paint on a curved surface. A horizontal dowel projecting from your work bench is very helpful, as you can insert this in your vase and it will support its weight, leaving both hands free. You also might find it easier to have more than two firings for each design.

The flower stalks and leaves radiate from the rocks, helping to dramatise the frightened posture of the bird.

Round box with a flower garland

I reduced the design and moved the two lower birds slightly towards the centre to fit better in the circle of the lid.

Paint the birds and the group of flowers before you do the ring of flowers and leaves. I used the spray for the front and back of the base of the box and linked them with the same garland as on the lid. I finished with a band of burnishing gold on the lid and the base at the second firing.

Monochrome design

During the eighteenth century in France the production of porcelain was forbidden except by the Vincennes (later called Sevres) factory. This prohibition was partially lifted in 1766, allowing other factories to make it providing it was clearly marked and decorated in blue (as was traditional in China) or in shades of one colour. Hence the popularity of such monochrome designs.

Remember that not only has a single-colour design a long tradition and is very beautiful in its own right, but you can select its colour to match your own furnishing scheme. The single colour does draw attention more to the painting skill, or lack of it, so take extra care.

Any of the designs in this book can be treated in this way. Just choose several tints and shades and apply as for the polychrome designs. Thicker applications of the colour will give you a darker and richer colour, but do make sure that there is plenty of contrast between the light and shade or it will look very flat. Shading is even more important than in polychrome designs. Also, leave some white areas to indicate where light falls.

The whole of a monochrome design can be finished in one firing, but you may well prefer to do it in two stages, as with a coloured design, leaving the fine detail and shading for the second firing.

By using the darkest shade to complete the decoration on the handles, foot and rim, it gives the design a frame. I finished with a line of platinum around both edges of the blue on rim, foot and handles, and fired it for a third time at 760°C/1400°F.

Hummingbirds on a fluted dish

This is quite a complicated and detailed piece, and it is best tackled in three firings. As I wanted to do this design on an oval plate, I slightly reduced the size of the leaves at the top, to make it fit better in the space. I also added the butterfly in the space above the central bird. At the same time as the last colour firing, I painted the pink shading in the fluted edge of the dish, using my large pointer brush with a shaded load.* Finally I painted the gold lines inside and on the rim with burnishing gold for a third firing.

* A shaded load, as you will remember from my first book, is when you spread the brush open as you enter the paint sideways, making a C shape with the brush. The load of paint will be visible on the top left of your brush (if you are right handed and entered your brush from the right). You make a similar action as you apply the paint to the china, so the darker load comes off the brush on one side, and a paler one on the other. This technique of painting emphasises beautifully the fluting on the dish.

Two birds by a stream

This design can easily be adapted for a round dish by moving the sprays of flowers away from the design, and slightly curving the landscape. The relief dots can be placed on the inside or outside edge of the rim, according to taste.

Paint the birds, landscape and flowers, and fire to 780°C/1435°F. For the second firing, finish the details on the birds and landscape. Then apply the relief enamel dots. Cover the enamel with a wide band of bright or burnishing gold for the third firing to 740°C/1360°F.

Gilded design on a squared vase

I reduced the design, then split it to fit on three of the four faces of the vase. I first painted the design with an even coat of burnishing gold, using a large brush (to avoid streaks). You can also carefully sponge the gold lightly before it dries to get an even surface. I then added a band of gold to the top and bottom of the vase. It was then fired at 780°C/1435°F.

Without burnishing the gold, I painted the details with a fine brush in a reddish-brown mixed with turps and fat oil (or a water-based medium), and fired it again to 780°C/1435°F. I lastly burnished the gold.

Birds on a trellis

This is a rather grand and ornate piece, and not very easy to paint on. I devised this design to fit the wide base and narrowing neck, and used part of the trellis for the lid.

Paint the birds first, then the trellis. When doing the trellis pay particular attention to the weave of the branches over and under each other, emphasising the shading on the dark side of the stems.

For the gilding, I again followed the shape of the piece, by adding small strokes to accentuate the ridges and grooves on the body and lid. Do not use too much gold or it will look heavy.

Birds on bamboo

After the birds had been painted, but before the second firing, I painted the 'V' shapes on the edge of the dish with a shaded load (see page 46) in the same brown as the border, to tie in with the bamboo.

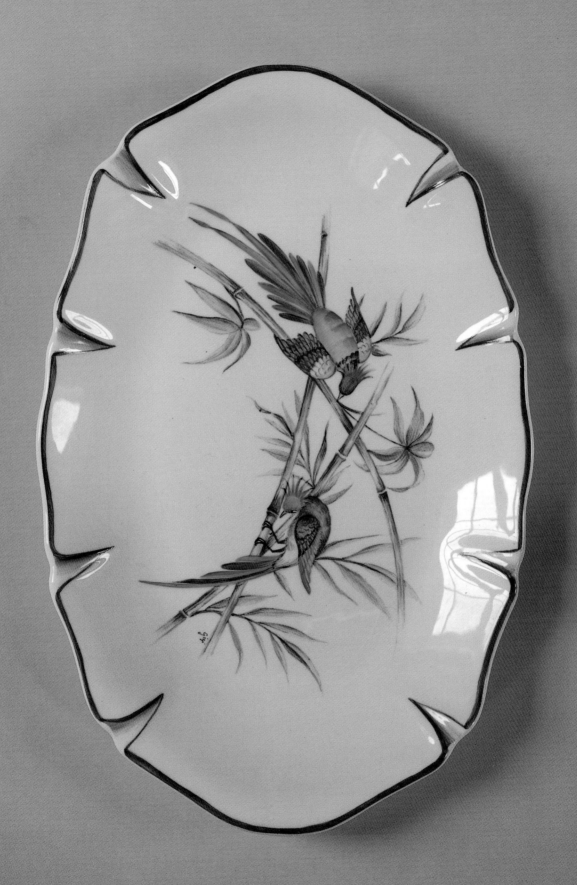

64

Two birds on a small vase

It is important to place the design carefully on this vase, so the top bird 'points' to the high point of the wavy rim. It would have been too heavy to have the same design on the other side, so I placed several pretty flying insects of my own invention around the vase. The gold rim adds the usual professional touch.

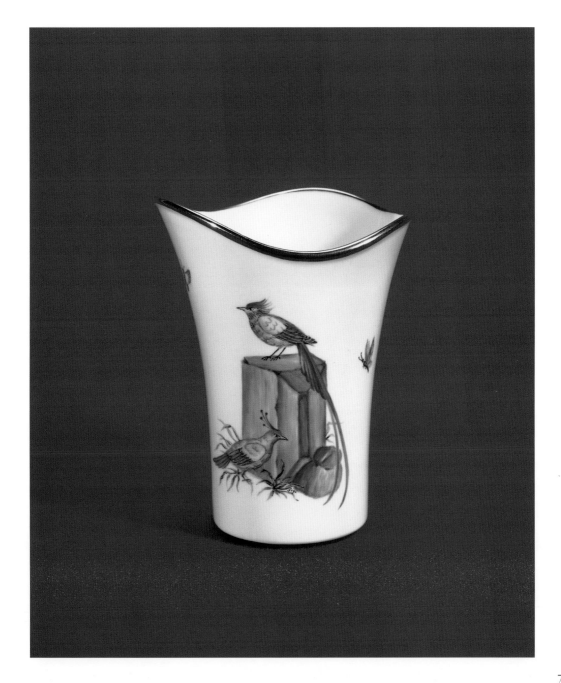

Peacock on a ribbon plaque

This thin porcelain plaque would make a great card for a wedding, anniversary or birthday, with initials, a name or even a message carefully written on the centre of the ribbon. If you want samples of ornamental initials, see my first book, page 83, or look at embroidery, cake decoration or typography books.

For those used to painting in a naturalistic way, the ribbon should be no trouble. It is just a matter of blending the colours so as to produce convincing shading. You will need several firings to keep the soft shading. The birds themselves are straightforward to paint.

Two birds on a log

Start with the wood behind the birds, using a pen and a darkish brown (mixed with icing sugar and water) for the rings and a colour wash of yellowish-brown for the oil medium. Then paint the birds. At the second firing add more wash to the wood and detail to the birds.

I continued the wood effect on the base of the box, to match the lid, then added the gold in a scalloped pattern on the curved edge, and put a spot near the base of the triangle, to make the box look like a fan.

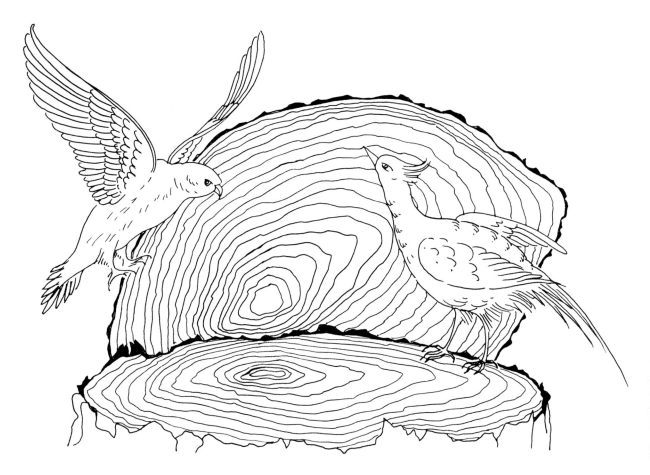

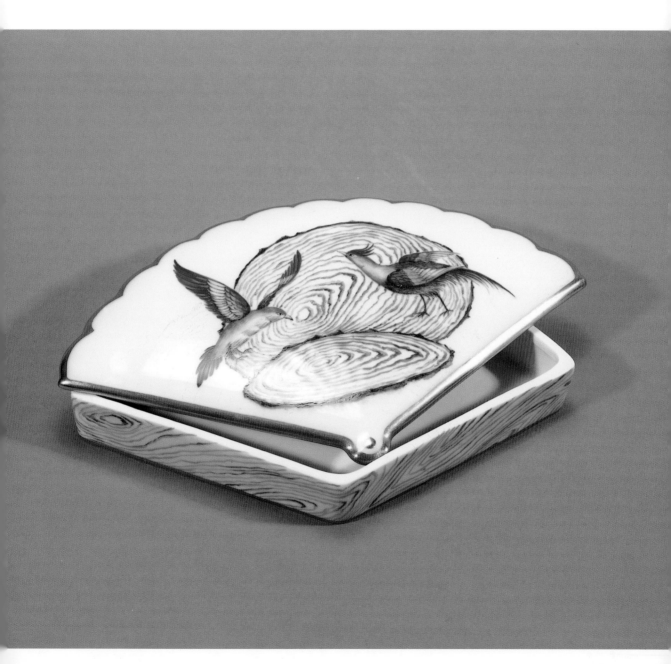

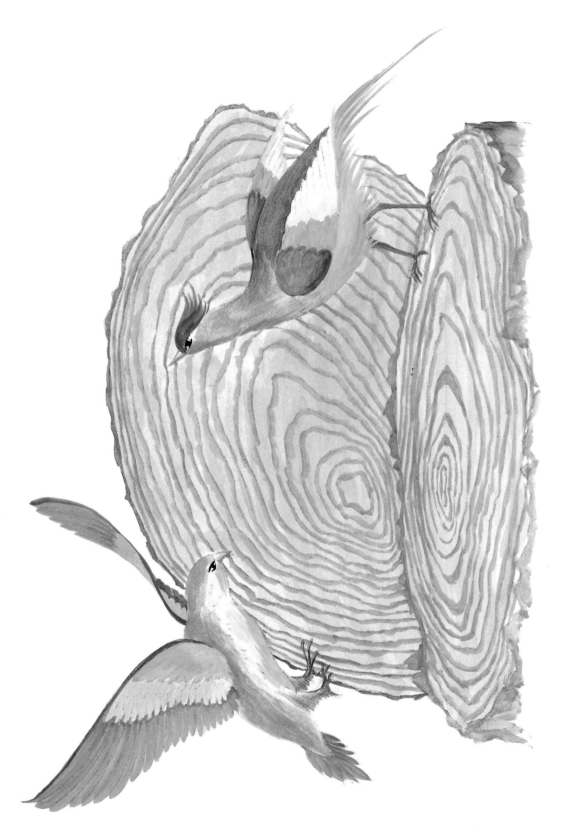

Hummingbirds on a Limoges box

Paint the birds first in one or two firings at 780°C/1435°F. I added a third bird (taken from the design on page 47). Then add the relief enamel with a brush (you can use the ready-prepared kit enamel if you wish) for the third firing, at 760°C/1400°F. I added a touch of pink to the enamel to make it clearly visible when fired. I continued the relief pattern on the sides of the base.

Cover the relief enamel with burnishing or bright gold for a final firing at 740°C/1360°F.

Octagonal plate with garland

I used masking fluid to reserve the central area and the four arched 'windows' in the wide rim before applying the pale yellow-green groundlay. This was fired at 800°C/1470°F.

With the central design, the first thing to paint is the ring, leaving out the birds and nest. Paint it light green all over then wipe out the area for the ribbon and the flowers. You can now paint the orange ribbon and the flowers at the same time as the birds and nest, or leave them for another firing. The four little birds in the panels were done at the same time as the central birds, in two firings, at 800°C/1470°F and 780°C/1435°F.

The burnishing gold was painted on and fired at 760°C/1400°F.

Round vase with flowers and rocks

Like the design on page 34, this curved vase
is a challenging but rewarding piece. Paint
the rocks first, then the flowers, then the
birds. Again, a gold rim finishes the design
perfectly.

China painters' associations and magazines

Britain

British China and Porcelain Artists Association (BCPAA)
Magazine: *The British China Painter*
Editor: Pat Norman, 2 Russet Drive, York, YO3 OPD Tel 01904.416066

Westfield House China Painting School
Magazine: *The British Porcelain Artist*
Editor: Celia Shute, Westfield House, North Avenue, Wakefield, West Yorkshire, WF1 3RX Tel 01924.360625 Fax. 01924.374477

Scotland

Scottish Association of Porcelain Artists
Contact: Lillian Skedd, 4 Irvine Terrace, Pitlochry, PH16 5HW
Tel 01796 472151

Ireland

Irish Association of Porcelain Artists
Contact: Maeve Spotswood, 24 Sidmonton Court, Bray, Co. Wicklow, Eire
Tel (00353) 12829551

There are many regional groups. For a full list write to the BSPAA at the address above

Italy

Magazine: *L'Arte della Porcellana*
IPAT contact: Donatella Viggiani, 13 via PL da Palestrina, Milan 20124
Tel (0039) 2.66981271
Fax (0039) 2.66981812

France

Association: AFADER
14 Residence Flotte, 18 Impasse de la Frescoule, 13008 Marseille

Germany

Association: FPMG
IPAT contact: Ulle Schmidt Ibach, Koenigsbergerstr. 34, D-8046 Garching b, Munich

Netherlands

Association: Het Porselein Schilder, Genootschap, Postbus 84, 9470 AB Zuidlaren
Contact: Jane Brandehof, Utrechtseweg 434, 6865 CP Doorwerth

Norway

Magazine: *Porcelens Maling*
Contact Editor: Helene Lovenskiold, N-2260 Kirkenier
Tel. (0047) 62941566. Fax. (0047) 62941170

USA

International Porcelain Art Teachers Inc (IPAT)
Magazine: *Porcelain Artist*
IPAT Executive Offices, 7424 Greenville Avenue, Suite 101, Dallas, Texas 75231

Australia

Australia Porcelain Art Teachers (APAT)
Magazine: *The Australian Porcelain Decorator*
Editor: Josephine Robinson, APDA Head Office, PO Box 156, Walkerville, South Australia 5081
Tel. (0061) 8.83441688
Fax (0061) 8.83448438

New Zealand

New Zealand Porcelain Artists Association
Magazine: *Onglaze*
Editors: Gay Carroll & Patricia Waitcombe, PO Box 1102, Palmerston North

South Africa

Porcelain Painters Association of Southern Africa (PPASA)
Magazine *South African Porcelain Painter*
Editor: Yochi Silove, PO Box 41535, Craighall 2024

Suppliers

Britain

R J Edge, 158 Star & Garter Road,
Lightwood, Stoke on Trent, ST4 3EN
Tel 01782.312700   Fax 01782.598114

Held Products, 16 Station Parade,
Harrogate, HG1 1UE
Tel 01423.504772   Fax 01423.528588

Lalco Ltd, 4 Eising Street, Fenton, Stoke on
Trent, ST4 2PR
Tel 01782.844858   Fax 01782.744501

France

Manufacture L Reine (white porcelain)
BP35, 87500 St Yrieix-La-Perce
Tel (0033) 5.55083600
Fax (0033) 5.55083609

Chastagner (white porcelain)
20 Avenue des Casseaux, F-878003
Limoges
Tel (0033) 5.55334574
Fax (0033) 5.55325958

Ceradel (China painting supply)
17-23 rue Frederic Bastiat, BP 1598, 87022
Limoges Cedex 9   Tel (0033) 5.55350235
Fax (0033) 5.55350230

Atelier 'Arts Ceramiques' (Supplies)
Les Mogets, Loisin, 74140 Douvaine
Tel (0033) 4.50943048

Italy

Hobbyceram, via PL da Palestrina 13,
20124 Milan
Tel. (0039) 2.66981271
Fax (0039) 2.66981812

Switzerland

Schira (Suplies and Seminars), Rue de
Bourg 25, 1003 Lausanne

Cercle Artistique Des Peintres sur
Porcelaine (Supplies and Seminars)
Rodolphe and May Noetzli, Evole 50, 2000
Neuchatel   Tel (0041) 32.7311986
Fax (0041) 32.7312016

Denmark

A/S Scjerning's Farver, Oster Alle, Posbox
119, 8400 Ebeltoft

Finland

Oy Handmade Ab (Supplies and
magazine), Sinooperi, Martinkylantie 41,
Fin 01720 Vantaa

USA
The Good Stuff (formerly China
Warehouse), 4919 E. 38th Avenue, Denver
CO 80207-1007   Tel (001) 303.3776008
Fax (001) 800.3776009

The House of China, PO Box 6835,
Louisville, Kentucky 40206
Tel (001) 502.4914628
Fax (001) 502.4919688

Maryland China Co, 54 Main Street,
Reistertown, Maryland 211136-0307
Tel (001) 410.8335559
Fax (001) 410.8331851

Rynne China, 222 W 8 Mile Road, Hel
Park, MI 488030   Tel (001) 800.4681987
Fax (001) 313.5420047

Haggerty Studio, PO Box 27491,
Minneapolis, MN 55427
Tel (001) 612.5597244
Fax (001) 612.5509653

Australia
The Gilberton Gallery, 101 Walkerville
Terrace, Walkerville, SA 5081
Tel (0061) 8.83441688
Fax (0061) 8.83448438

New Zealand
Shand China Co, 30 Waldegrave Street,
Palmerston North
Tel & Fax (0064) 6.3550509

South Africa
The Clay Pot, PO Box 51151, Radene 2124
Tel (0027) 11.6407316/4860
Fax (0027) 4851672

Design for a heart-shaped box

This is a very pretty box, and makes a lovely present. The base is not visible here, and in any case not seen very much from the top, but I treated it as a piece on its own, with the rope design all around the heart shape. You can use a pen to outline the rope before colouring it in, as this might make the twists clearer. To link the two parts together I painted a band of gold around both edges, on the second firing.